# Entangled

# Hearts

By

Why Yet

*Entangled Hearts*

# ENTANGLED HEARTS

Copyright © 2015 Why Yet

All rights reserved. No part of this book may be reproduced or transmitted in any form or by any means, electronic or mechanical, including photocopying, recording, or by any information storage and retrieval system, without permission in writing from the publisher. All questions and/or request are to be submitted to: 134 Andrew Drive, Reidsville NC, 27320.

To the best of said publisher knowledge, this is an original manuscript and is the sole property of author **WHY YET**

Printed in the United States of America

**ISBN-13:978-0692550755**
**ISBN-10:0692550755**

Printed by Createspace 2015
Published by BlaqRayn Publishing Plus 2015
**\*\*Original text © 2006 by Markisha Bunn**
   **First printing by Publish America**

Entangled Hearts

# *Dedication*

For all who dare to love with hearts wide open... This book is dedicated to everyone who has ever fallen in love, been hurt by love or found true love... Music is the kiss of life and love is its dance

To D.C.B. - thank you for being you. To Mom - I exist because you gave me the chance to, thank you. To D.B.3. - Thank you for encouraging me to find my voice and to use it. To V.L.B. - Thank you for unknowingly encouraging me to publish this collection the first time; To S.M.M. – Thank you for encouraging me to find me and to be happy with me for me. To A.Y.B. – Thank you for encouraging me to blow the dust off of my pad and pen and get to writing again. To B.M.M. and B.J.O. - Thank you for inspiring my work. To Ms. Evon DeBrow, Ms. Virginia Lam, Ms. Snyder, Mrs. Smith, Ms. Davis and everyone who encouraged me to push past my potential, THANK YOU!

Entangled Hearts

## *Contents*

*Meeting:* 1-12

*Falling:* 13-41

*Hurting:* 42-61

*Healing:* 62-79

# Entangled Hearts

By

Why Yet

*Entangled Hearts*

# *Meeting:*

*We met when our eyes locked and chemistry began...*

*Entangled Hearts*
# On the Local

Dark, brooding eyes
Beneath a furrowed brow
Mulling over deep thoughts…
Smooth, chocolate skin
Gracing a broad nose
Relaxed on his face, his
Cheekbones tell of strength
That boils in his blood
From generations past.
Lips, so full and plump,
(A caramelized cocoa)
Enticing,
Beckoning me to him.
Lips that look soft and tender,
The urge to gently bite one
And draw it into my mouth is overwhelming.
The train shudders to a halt
And opens the doors
Letting this chocolate work of art
Escape my vision…

*Entangled Hearts*
# Heart Petals

     My heart petals open
Slowly to your touch
Like the warm rays of the sun
Melting away ice
After winter's brutal force.
     My heart petals open
To your soft spoken words
Carried on clouds of love
And rainbows of joy.
     My heart petals open
At your intense stare
Looking within
Past the pain I bear
     My heart petals open
At the mere sight of you
Blooming wild and fragrant
In a field of dandelion dangers
And petunia strangers
Wafting in my breeze
Aching to distract my attention
From you…

*Entangled Hearts*
# Comfort Zone

You are my comfort zone,
      My night light in the dark
      Since you encourage me
           Even in my fear.

You are my comfort zone,
      My spiritual nexus
      In the midst of chaos
      When you vibe with me
           Through voice-mail.

You are my comfort zone,
      Because you give me space to be
      No demands,
      No expectations,
      Because with you
           I am free.

*Entangled Hearts*
# Un-chartered Waters

Gentle, soothing notes
Quieting my mind
As the soft, sweet chocolate
Caresses my senses…
My spirit wavering between
Here and sweet memories
Of a tenderness that I craved;
A yearning within awakens
And the sensation frightens me.
My emotions swiftly changing,
Transitioning into something beautiful
But I am not ready.
I am not prepared for this.
What am I doing?
Allowing my inner self
To speak full truths
Unveiling my raw feelings, my vulnerability,
And fear grips me tightly…

*Entangled Hearts*
# A Pleasant Surprise

Briefly reconnecting
After several years' pause
And a pleasant surprise awaited me…
Your confession
Of attraction
Sent me reeling
In a whirlwind of emotions
Full of crimsoned cheeks
                         And moistened sweetness…

*Entangled Hearts*
# The Artistry

A smooth, chocolate covered canvas
Encasing deep set eyes
Full of intriguing thoughts
Spanning an abyss of memories
Covering all senses.
A broad nose that catches the faintest
Of scents,
Subtle as a summer's breeze
Felt by the gentle stirring of the hairs
On your skin;
Cheekbones that grace the smile
That spreads sunshine upon all
Who are graced by it.
A smile completed by full sensuous lips
Drawing attention with every syllable spoken;
Spoken from a slender neck
That gives way to strong, broad shoulders.
Strengthened to help carry the burden
Of the world
With that one mate destined to walk
His path with him.
Muscular arms to enclose and protect
While a wide chest provides comfort
And a waist made simply to be held
By the most tender of female hands.
Strong hips and thighs, formed like
That of a mighty thoroughbred
Steed,
Divinely crafted for sensuous thrusting.
His member, bobbing patiently
Waiting for a chance to fulfill its duty

### *Entangled Hearts*

In pleasure before giving way
To solid knees, sensitive calves and kingly feet
Molded to withstand many obstacles.
The artistry in which this magnificent
Creature was created,
Is a visual treat.

*Entangled Hearts*
# Dreams

But dreams will stay dreams
If you don't believe
In the realness of the visions
That you have just seen…
FEAR is false evidence appearing real
If you love her then tell her
What's the big deal?
Shedding light on your true emotional state
Is scary but releases
Unnecessary weight
From your mind…
In time to the rhythm,
Right at the start
Take a deep breath
And speak from your heart…

*Entangled Hearts*
# What Have You Done To Me?

I
Can't sleep
Because your voice
Resonates inside my mind
Sending spastic waves of warmth
Throughout my inner core.

I
Can't think
Because echoes
Of your spoken thoughts
Swim throughout my psyche
Creating the most sensuous images
Causing a dampness
Like never before,
Yet you are miles away.

I
Smile – a lot
Because the heat building inside
Wants to erupt
In passionate waves
Rolling through me
And into you,
Caressing you in my
Sensuous glory,
Basking in an afterglow
That can only be –
Heavenly…
What have you done to me?

*Entangled Hearts*
# Sound Waves

I could see the intensity in his eyes
As he gazed into mine.
I could feel the heated passion passing
Between us like air;
Yet could do nothing.
Paralyzed by a need to be closer to this man
A need I have never before experienced
A need stronger than hunger
Yet deeper than thirst and
Then he leaned toward me slowly
And whispered softly in my ear.
Sending shock waves through my senses,
Electric currents down my spine
Tickling my nipples, spreading warmth
To my belly and ending as a pulsating
Shudder down in my sweet spot,
The spot that will forever be his…

*Entangled Hearts*
# Seduced By You

Caught unexpectedly
Unaware of your deeply
penetrating stare,
I was seduced by you…

      An innocent touch of the hand
      sent shock waves throughout
      my entirety,
      while your words caressed my mind
      for time eternal…

            A kiss, so innocent yet promising
            love's heights to soar
            beyond that third floor bench…

**Entangled Hearts**

# *Falling:*

*The wind rushes up to greet me as I find myself falling… in love.*

*Entangled Hearts*
# Untitled

You touched my hand
And electricity surged through me
You looked into my eyes
And my soul flew free
You kissed my lips
And my spirit danced
You spoke my name
And my heart sang

# Innocent Discretion

Your look,
disarming.
Your smile,
alarming.
Your words,
intoxicating.
Your touch,
arousing.
An innocent discretion
that creates life
in memories
that birth love
with each remembrance…

*Entangled Hearts*
# Smiling

As I stand in your doorway
Listening intently
To the beautifully orchestrated words
Of adoration
Pouring from your heart
Forming a protective halo around me…
Smiling
I see the warm glow of love in your eyes,
Eyes that have penetrated my barriers
And invaded my hurt filled space
Softening my armor…
Smiling
As you stand before me
Outstretched hand
Expressing your feelings
For me to understand
And behold
Your sensuality…
Smiling
Because I see love in its true form
Before me
Uncloaked, unmasked
Clearly grabbing my full attention
When you slowly tilt my chin
And kiss me softly…

*Entangled Hearts*
# Your Fragrant Bloom

Skin soft and satiny,
Like the petals of a rose
Accepting of the love you lavish
Upon my entity
Like a cool spring rain
Quenching a thirst
I had not realized was there;
Watering my spirit
Sowing your love seeds
Into my very soil
With words that
Intoxicate beautifully
Leaving me
In a love-filled stupor
Looking and waiting,
Eager for my next poetic fix
Leaving the faintest tint of blush
Throughout my face
As my seductive fragrance
Permeates the atmosphere
Around us…

*Entangled Hearts*
# Midnight

Full moon shining
Lighting rippled waves of the river.
The stars' reflections twinkle in the water.
Whispering as I
Look into your eyes,
They are full like the moon
Shining bright with a love
So deep
As you lean in and kiss me softly.
Tasting the lips that whispered love
Into your ear
Forever tickling your heart
At midnight.

*Entangled Hearts*
# Sailing

Sailing,
Drifting in the sea
Of mixed emotions.
Not confused,
But infused with the spirit
Of loving you.
Infused with a hope
Of being with you.
Infused with the courage
Of sailing after you
Because in the end
I sail for you…

*Entangled Hearts*

# Rest With Me

Baby just lay your head on my chest
Get some much needed rest
As I caress the nape of your neck
Feeling your stress…
Breathe in rhythm with me
My king
My mate
My husband who equates my being
By being my protector
My friend
My lover
Until the end of time –
I am here for you
To ease the temperament of your mind
After time external caused infernal
Interruptions of our synergic flow…
Baby I know
So just lay right here
Relax
Recharge
Relive and
Re-love
Our reunion.

*Entangled Hearts*
# Love's Light

I am humbled
By your simplistic admissions of love;
Your search for and acceptance of love
As she is.
Do not worry,
Love will not pass you by.
She waits patiently for you
As you search ardently for her
And I am she.
I am the light and love you seek;
A brilliant reflection
Of your spiritual nature
That shines bright
Like a beacon for me to follow.
A warm glow of loving light
Emitting from your eyes,
Your heart,
And your soul.
I feel it and it is calling me home…

*Entangled Hearts*

# What Is Love?

Love is that beautiful song
That triggers a warm sensation
All over your body.

Love is that movie
You can watch over and over,
Yet never tire of it.

Love is the perfect spring day
Where the birds sing,
The flowers bloom and
The sun lends just enough warmth
For the air to be just right.

Love is that hot bubble bath
After a hard day.

Love is light.
Love… just is.

*Entangled Hearts*
# My Soul Wants To Sing

My soul wants to sing,
  Notes of love, hurt and growth
    Because my spirit says so.

My soul wants to sing,
  Because my spirit has been inspired
    By so many;
      Lauryn, Erykah, Whitney, Anita, Sade, Alicia…
        The list drags on
          For as long as I remember their names and
            Notes that imprinted on and impressed me.

My soul wants to sing,
  So the universe can feel my hurt
    And my love
      Because my spirit speaks to me that way.

My soul wants to sing
  Because my spirit needs to.

*Entangled Hearts*
# Inspire Me

Raise me up,

                Lift me high,

                                Inspire me

To reach for the

                                Highest cloud

Or search for the

                                Deepest sea

Or paint the

                              Most brilliant picture

Or sing the

                                Sweetest song

Or make the

                              Most passionate love

            That can be inspired by another.

*Entangled Hearts*
# Soft Kisses

Light, feathery kisses
That graces my skin
Peppering it with goose bumps
In expectation of more…
        My forehead tingles
       From the tenderness passed
      Between your lips and my skin
          Starting a fever
                That is never-ending…
                  My cheeks burn
                With the flame of love
                 That trickles down
                 Following the heat
                   Of your kisses…
                  My lips soften
         In acceptance of your tenderness,
        Your softness,
        Your warmth
Succumbing to the loving
Sure to follow your
Soft kisses…

*Entangled Hearts*
# Dancing

You watch as my hips sway
In time to the rhythm of the drums;
My heart's pace racing to keep up,
Feeling your love's heat
And my passion's intensity.
I spin and dance
Urging you to join me
Become one with me
So the drum beats
Will beat rhythmically
Together with us...

*Entangled Hearts*
# Sweet Sentiments

The sweetest sentiments
Pour from your lips
Like a honey-dew kiss
Sweet, light and irresistible.
Baby hold on
Because I am on THE way;
Thinking about your smile,
Your eyes, and
Your thighs
Pushing up against mine
All day.
I watch the clock closely;
Embraced at the door,
Clothes hitting the floor,
Loving until sore
All over,
Damn…

*Entangled Hearts*
# The Morning After...

I stretch...
          A yawn escapes my lips
          As your scent lingers in my senses
          Awakening every particle
          Of my being...
I look for you...
          And on your side of the bed
          Find a written note
          Scented in your love
          Describing the joy and ecstasy
          You enjoyed last night...
I smile towards the door...
          Imagining the direction you travel
          As you think of my sensuous body
          Wrapped tightly in your arms,
          An embrace warmer than Arizona heat
          Yet comforting like an angel's touch
          And I love you more,
          Miss you more,
          Anticipating when you will return
          So the anthem we have started
          Can be completed...
A moan escapes me...
          As my mind drifts on the heights I've reached,
          The mountains you've peaked
          And the sheets you've streaked
          With the flowing juices
          Of our intermingled passion;
          Becoming aroused again
          I slip your pillow softly between my warm thighs
Waiting for your return...

*Entangled Hearts*
# Loving Your Beauty

In my spirit I flow in your direction
Because your heart is my compass
Guiding me towards your warm light of passion;
Glowing embers
That reflect the love we have for each other;
It is reflected in your eyes when I gaze
Truly amazed
At how regal you appear to me;
Looking down upon your face
When I assume
My favorite place on top.
Staring as you enjoy
The wondrous curves of my body
That I sway and move to your rhythm,
Your song,
Your dance
Because
The way you love
And adore
Has me in your trance
And
If your hair shriveled,
Skin wrinkled, and
Eyes glazed over
I would love you still
Because you are my king,
Handsome and strong
With your love boiling over
Into my honey pot…

*Entangled Hearts*
# Surprise Visit

The way you held me close
As you bit softly into my neck
Caused spasms of pleasure
To course through me.
Staring into my eyes
You caused me to blush
And look away from your closeness.
Relaxed,
I glance over your sensuous body,
Chiseled over time
And being perfected each day
When your sudden penetration
Jolted me out of my trance.
Divine pleasure swam through my loins
Causing a dam to burst
And rivers of tears to flow from my eyes
As ecstasy claims me.
Guttural moans erupt forth
And a warmth envelops me
As I grip your body close
Inviting you in further,
Wanting you to explore deeper
As only you can…

*Entangled Hearts*
# Inside

       Inside,
I am like a warm furnace
Fueled by your tender passions…
       Erupting,
Like a dormant volcano
Under your enticing touch;
       Inside,
I am liquid fire.
I singe your steeled wood
Yet it pleases you to see me this way.
I allow emotions
To direct the flow of motion
       Between us,
Riding through us
Like an ocean wave.
Crashing against our shore
Of heated passions
Unspoken,
       Yet signaled
By ascended knees
Languid tongue
And well placed hands between us.
With you inside…
       I will be pleased.

*Entangled Hearts*
# Your Heart's Song

Your heart's song
Has a beautiful melody;
One that vibrates inside of me
    Quietly,
        Soothing,
            And intoxicating.
I understand you clearly
Since your heart is singing
In tune with my own
Joining together
To create a more beautiful melody,
A melody of you and me…
    Sing on,
        Sing loud,
           Sing love.

*Entangled Hearts*
# I Step Closer

I step closer,

Gingerly awaiting the secrets
Of your innermost chamber;
The very thoughts you kept hidden
For so long
I imagined they vanished.
So to bring them back
I opened my heart,
Exposed my joy
And shared them with you
To nourish and fulfill…

I step closer, a little eager now

For your eyes
Are shining in the bright light
Of the moon
Anticipating
My reaction to your hearts' secrets;
Love reborn
Out of hurt,
The best form
Because the heart
Now rejoices
In finding another
Who mirrors itself
Shining bright and full
Of loving life
Awaiting the moment to share together…
For your love I step closer.

*Entangled Hearts*
# Dance of Dreams

The dance of dreams
Lasting for infinity
Locked together in an embrace
That rivals a nature made blending;
Causing the seas to roar
And the oceans to crash
In a jealous rage
For what we have created
Between us
Has a resonance
Beautiful enough
To truly be called
Love's song.
Musically enhanced embraces,
Leaving traces
Of our sensuous signature
Everywhere we step.

*Entangled Hearts*
# Un Amore

Les oeils de toi.
Les mains de toi.
Les bras de toi.
Tres bon.

>     You infuse my soul
>       With a love
>      I can not shake
>     Nor do I want to.

Les oeils de toi.
Les mains de toi.
Les bras de toi.
Tres bon.

>    I wish to embrace your love
>           And float
>      Within that warm bubble
>    That courses through my heart.

Les oeils de toi.
Les mains de toi.
Les bras de toi.
Tres bon.
Je t'aime beaucoup
Parce que tu es mon amore.

*Entangled Hearts*
# Addicted to Love

Okay.
      I admit it.
           I am addicted to love.

The same way
      I am addicted to chocolate.

         Nothing soothes
Like that warm feeling inside.

*Entangled Hearts*
# Mind Blown

You spoke in baritone timbres
About your life's passions
With fire in your eyes
That hypnotized me.
You stared into my
Being
Looking at me completely
Soulfully undressing the
Layers of my mind
Caressing my thoughts
From behind
Kissing my dreams
And massaging my
Fears until
Speaking soft and slow
So no one would know
How your mind blowing
Love
Has me embalmed
In your essence.

*Entangled Hearts*
# Love You So

What is it about you
That makes me love you so?
A question I need not ask
Because it is your spirit
Which reflects the goodness in my spirit
And sparkles when I look into your eyes;
It is the sincerity in your heart
That sings to my heart
Twinkling in your voice when we talk;
It is your compassion for the world
And your complete acceptance
Of me as I am
That makes me love you so.

*Entangled Hearts*
# Forever and Always

Forever and always
A love so deep
The passion spills forth from your eyes
And words have yet to pass your lips.
Your beauty intoxicates me like a fine wine
On a warm summer day
With remnants of your kisses lingering,
Re-igniting a fire
Deep within.
Taunting and teasing me
Until I recapture the ecstasy
That was us
Forever and always…

*Entangled Hearts*
# Enchantment

Whispers of a subtle voice
Full of bass
Commanding yet not controlling
Strong and powerful
But not overbearing…
You gaze into my eyes
Drinking in my soul
Absorbing the secrets hidden within my core.
I am trapped in that magnetic gaze
So many emotions exchanged.
Slowly you lean closer and softly graze my lips
With your own,
My heart flutters and a fire surges
Through me;
The flame, beginning at my lips and
Traveling quickly downward
Engorging my nipples,
Tingles warmly gliding
Down my spine
And exploding within my vulva
Releasing my natural satin liquid…

*Entangled Hearts*

# Joy

If I could explain the joy I feel
There would be no need for poetry.
My physical words
Would convey all the love
That lay within my heart and soul
Rendering love songs obsolete.
Formulas and equations could not calculate
The exquisite taste of life
I experience in your company.

# *Hurting:*

*Crushed and winded I feel as the ground
opens wide its arms to receive me…*

*Entangled Hearts*
# Heart Paths

Following this path
That my heart lay before me
Challenging,
    Taunting,
        And teasing,
Begging me to follow in the footsteps
Of my soul's whisper
    Until it leads me
        To you.

*Entangled Hearts*
# Misplaced Love

Love,
So bright and warm,
Beautifully sweet
And comforting
Filling my heart with immense joy

But
As my teary eyes refocus
I realize I have been giving my love to one
While my heart belongs to another.

Has too much time passed to correct this?
My heart aches with each passing day
Because the one I love is not here
Yet I still try to share love with the other;

But it feels so wrong,
It is wrong
And resentment begins to breed
Because my love has been misplaced.

*Entangled Hearts*

# Invested

I invested my time, my heart and my mind
Only to rear back with wounds and scars
Inflicted then reflected
Inspected and suspected
Accused, misused, and abused
I invested my heart
When yours was parked
In a closed off garage – reserved for another
Driver
While you pointed your accusations at me
    - without cause
Screaming and stomping to drown out the truth
Of my words, the honesty of my tears
Reflective of the years I have invested
And for what?

# Patience

There is a sad song in my heart
For time will not tell me
How long it will be
'Fore I may lay eyes
Upon your face once more.
The very face that brings
Smiles in my dreams
And peace to my eyes,
The very face who
Beholds my heart
And my soul
Yet we have only 'loved'
In my dreams, so
There is a sad song in my heart
For time will not tell me
How long it will be
'Fore I may lay eyes
Upon your face once more.

*Entangled Hearts*
# Still, Yet

I care for you
   Still, yet
      I have fallen out
         Still, yet
            I stay for you
               Still, yet
                  I have fallen out
                     Still, yet
                        I comfort you
                     Still, yet
                  I have fallen out
               Still, yet
            I am here for you
       But,
      I have fallen
   Out
Of love with you.

*Entangled Hearts*
# That Night

She lay there, in the dark
Unfulfilled.
Watching the tick of the clock
As the minutes drift on
Measuring the timelessness
She experiences
Unfulfilled.
He sweats and moans
In her ear
Lavishing her with empty words
And caresses
As she lay there
Unfulfilled,
Wishing it was done.
Her punishment – pain.

*Entangled Hearts*
# Longing

My soul hurts,

                Cries out in pain
                In a claustrophobic strain
                Of my existence here.

My soul cries,

                Lack of understanding
                My complex self
                Has left me bared,
                Half exposed.

My soul begs,

                For its other half
                To return
                As the moon
                Begs for the sun.

A union blended together
Like the hues of spring
And the scents of summer,
My soul longs for these things with you.

*Entangled Hearts*
# Love's Journey

Nervous glances and awkward smiles
Began our path to love.
Quiet talks and long walks
Comforted my heart.
Stolen kisses and soft caresses
Brightened my world where sadness lived
Then all went dark…
No more lovely walks,
Long talks,
Or stolen kisses.
Only sad tears
And aching pain filled my lonely nights.
Images of a different path…
Short talks occasionally
Is what we now have
Easing the pain and tears
That helped pave love's journey
Which is not complete…

*Entangled Hearts*
# The Abyss

This hurt,
A sad pain
Unlike any I ever felt before.
A gagging, suffocating sadness
That dwarfs all light and goodness.
A deep, dark abyss
Of depression.
A bottomless pit of regret,
Hurt and sadness.
So much pain
So many tears
Falling, flowing, shedding
Begging for the hurt to go.
Begging the hurt to take the sadness
And the tears
Far from me…

*Entangled Hearts*
# Sum of Seven

I thought you were my cure
For my sniffling,
Sneezing,
Crying,
Screaming,
Frustrated,
Heartbroken
And still loving him blues.
But you weren't
And I shouldn't have expected you to be anyways.
But you allowed me to hope and dream
That your love elixir
Would fix what was wrong with my heart.
Dangling me over the valley of forever
With promises of togetherness.
A love so tender,
At first,
Swelling my belly
With the sweet gift of life
Puffing your chest with pride and beaming eyes
Until reality set in
And I saw you begin
To shed the mask I had grown to love
For seven years.
A dam has ruptured
And my Niagara
Falls with salt filled tears
Knowing your love elixir,
Which was supposed to be a quick fixer –
Not a back street in the kitchen mix
Was a smokescreen.

*Entangled Hearts*

# Love Has Me

Love has me in a whirlwind of confusion
Exposing my heart and emotions
To one who…
Is unsure of what to do,
Unsure of what he wants,
Unsure…
Yet I love him more than ever
For his sincerity,
For the love I hear in his voice,
For the love I have seen
Burning in his eyes
Like candle flames.
I have stared love in the face and not blinked
So how am I supposed to walk away
To look for a new love
When the one who owns my heart
Still breathes?

*Entangled Hearts*

# Loss

My heart feels trampled and abandoned
Because of choices I made in the past.
My one true love is no longer mine
For to wed another he will.
My heart and soul cried out
In the most severe pain,
Deeper than I have ever felt
Knowing his love will forever be gone from me.
My body aches
As my soul mourns my loss.

*Entangled Hearts*
# Morning Dew

Tossed and turned
And turned and tossed
While thoughts in my mind ran wild.
Hurt and pain
Came to visit again
But my words fell on deaf ears –
AGAIN.
Tired, exhausted, worn down and worn out
I recognize the problem is me.
Trying to prove what is already evident in me.
My mistake
For seeing your hurt, your pain from the past
And trying to ease and appease your mind
So that we could last…

*Entangled Hearts*
# I Will Not

I
WILL
NOT
    Apologize for who I am;
    A blooming flower
    Opening up to the warming rays of the sun.

I
WILL
NOT
    Apologize for how I think;
    A mind forever searching
    To understand everything in my universe.

I
WILL
NOT
    Apologize for loving you;
    My heart opened, exposed, vulnerable
    And loving the way you made me feel.
    What I will apologize for
    Is using poor judgment
    In some of my decisions
    But,
I
WILL
NOT
    Apologize for being me.

*Entangled Hearts*
# Life Moves On

Life moves on
Dragging me
Kicking and screaming
Because
I can't turn my back
On a past
That
Will not claim me.
Life moves on
Pulling me
Across dirt roads
With scraped knees and
Bleeding wounds
Towards a mountain of change
That I resist
For fear of the unknown.
Life moves on
Through a thicket of thorns,
Hornets and bees
Sticking, stinging, and poking me
Until I realize
Change is inevitable
Because
Life continues on…

*Entangled Hearts*

# Funny

You ran and ran and ran
Around my emotions like quicksand
After asking for my attention and affection.
You played with my emotions
Like a hand of blackjack
Threw other females in my face,
Pushed my affection to the back
Like I was second rate.
Now I'm at the point where
I don't give a damn anymore
My feelings are raw and
My emotions are sore
But you want to try and blame ME
For the lack of intimacy
That YOU created
When you gave X, Y, Z your attention…
Funny.

*Entangled Hearts*
# Missed Train

Tears
Wash the dust from my face
As I watch the train pull away;
But the train I missed
Was not mine to catch…
A hand reaches out
Grasping a napkin
And offering to help;
Looking up with
Tear filled eyes
I am uplifted.
Another hand reaches out
Holding a mirror
And a face appears
In the reflection,
Mine.
I hear a voice,
Tender and soft,
In my ear:
"Dry your eyes baby. He hasn't realized
The beautiful gem
He left behind.
You didn't miss his train.
He missed yours."
I felt a small kiss
On my left cheek
Yet when I turned around
I was alone.

*Entangled Hearts*
# About Me

There is an inner strength inside
Which gets overlooked
By other's perception
Of my ability to handle MY pain.
Pain is no stranger to me
Be it physical or emotional;
Both becoming regular visitors
In one form or another.
Do I have a
"HANDLE WITH CARE"
Sign on my back?
If so,
Have you read it out loud?

**HANDLE.**                                      **WITH.**                                   **CARE.**

Not fear,
But truth, trust, honesty…
Need I go on?
I am resilient
Born of a line
Of tremendous strength
And I will not shatter easily…

*Entangled Hearts*
# Will Love Find Me

I run and hide
Because the love I had
Is gone from me.
I hide within
Behind my smile
Unsure of what is there.
My heart yearns
For that love I had before,
The calm and beauty
Of which I adored –
Him…
Will love find me
Although fear
Shrouds me in a cloud of doubt?
Will love find me
Although my heart
Seeks to reunite with the past?
Where do I go
To find strength and courage?
How do I move on?
When will I grow enough
To weather my emotional storms?
How will peace find me
With my soul restless?
My spirit stirs uneasily,
Pacing,
Anticipating the day
When love lives no longer,
Giving warmth to the belly of fear
That
Love will not find me.

# *Healing:*

*Out of the seed of pain, an understanding will grow into healing love's wounds...*

*Entangled Hearts*
# Random Thoughts V

The love that fills my heart,
The thoughts that crowd my head
Barely leave enough room to complete my daily tasks.
Your words make sense and touch me in that place
That loves and hurts.
They give me hope and take it away at the same time.
I wait for another message.
I pray for a phone call.
I hope to gain control of myself
So our friendship can blossom.
There are so many words I wish to say,
So many hugs I wish to give
But the boundaries of friendship prevent it.
The poem you sent was beautiful
And it almost brought tears to my eyes… but I thought why?
It's not like you died.
I have learned that life is love
And love is light,
So life is light – good and beautiful.

*Entangled Hearts*
# Writing Pains

This pen scratches feverishly
Across this white Savannah
Scarred with blue lines
And visions
Of stories
Yet to be told
Lives yet to be sold
Love yet to behold
In your mind's eye.

*Entangled Hearts*
# The Pages of My Life

As I look across the river
I glance over the pages of my life.
There are blank spots and ink smudges
In the spaces where uncertainty
Ruled my thinking,
Controlling my emotions
Creating lasting voids of hurt and guilt.

    As I look across the river
    I glance over the pages of my life
    Thinking of ways to correct the smudges
    And fill in the blank spots
    Erasing the hold uncertainty
    Has over me;
    Healing the hurt and sending away the guilt.

As I look across the river
I glance over the pages of my life
And think of how I want the next chapter to read
No blanks, no smudges, full of memories
And self-assurance.

*Entangled Hearts*
# Forgive Me

Forgive me Lord,
For I have sinned
So many times,
In so many ways
The biggest is not
Being able to forgive myself
For all of my mistakes…

Forgive me Lord,
For I have sinned
On my path to Glory.
I wish to hear your word
But fear grips my heart,
Fear of being alone…

Forgive me Lord,
For I have sinned
So many days
When I allowed doubt
To dictate my actions,
Ruling my heart and mind
Hurting,
Hurting me and you…

Forgive me Lord
For I have sinned
By not completely trusting
Your will for my life
And judging myself
And others…

### *Entangled Hearts*

Forgive me Lord,
For I have sinned
Giving all of my earthly love
To one who is not
You or I
Please…
Forgive me Lord
For I have sinned.

*Entangled Hearts*

# Winds Of Change

The winds of change are blowing around
Disturbing what once was settled
Raising the dormant wants and desires
Stirring up passionate moments,
Ideas flurrying
Fears scurrying, hiding from the light
The wind is allowing to filter in
By blowing out the night.

*Entangled Hearts*
# Here I Am

Here I sit
Lost in a trance of piano keys
And fountain waves
Captured by the beauty that surrounds me
Cloaking me in nature's protective hold.
Here I am
Open, wounded and willing
To let go of all that hurts me,
Of all that weakens me
Obscuring my vision
Of a purer love.
Here I am
Healing,
Smiling with all of the grace
Love has to give
For love blankets me
With her warmth
So that I may share it
With another…

*Entangled Hearts*
# Healing

Walking alongside the river
Feeling her calming presence.
The cool breeze of the wind on my face,
My soul rejoicing, feeling renewed
As if a longtime friend has come to visit;
The river is my longtime friend
And I have come to visit.
Now I feel my healing process
Truly begin.

*Entangled Hearts*
# Be True

Be true.
Not to me,
But to you.
Let that inner child come thru
And smile like the rays of the sun.
Running, jumping, sliding along
Happily
Until the day is done.
Let that inner self smile
While licking your favorite ice cream
In 98 degree heat.
Sucking the bottom of the cone
To keep your favorite confection
From dripping into the cement cracks
And when you turn your back…
Everyone's gone –
Your smile fades,
You raise your shades,
Eyes a little hazy,
Mind a little lazy,
Hair different shades of gray
As you remember your age,
65.
Damn –
Time flies
When you try
To be fly
Do or die
Reachin' for that
Pie in the sky
Livin' real high

## *Entangled Hearts*

Above your means
To befriend fiends
Who
Despise you anyway.
So why waste your time
Being defined
By their lives
When you can
Just be true
To you?

*Entangled Hearts*
# Self, I'm Sorry

Self,
I'm sorry I ignored you
When you warned me to steer clear
And keep my mind focused
On what I hold dear.

Self,
I'm sorry I neglected you
For the image of another
Who claimed
To love me better
Between falsehoods
And guises

Self,
I'm sorry I tuned you out
When expressing
What I wanted to believe as true
When all I needed
Was you.

Self,
I'm sorry.

*Entangled Hearts*
# Shout

Shout!
Release the flow of pent up
Aggression,
Irritation, and
Frustration.

Shout!!
Let all of the hurt and pain
Slide down your smooth cheeks
In that hot trail of tears.

SHOUT!!!
Let the cleansing tears
Refresh,
Rejuvenate, and
Replenish
Your strength
So you can continue
Your upward journey.

SHOUT!!!
So the heavens will hear
And hell will weep
For the strength and power
Being released
From your lungs
Letting go of your pain…

*Entangled Hearts*
# Keep Healing

It's alright babe,
A gift of innocence you gave
Feeling a spiritual high
When together,
A high only felt by you
But
How much stronger have you become
In spite of it all
Feeling love,
Being hurt by love
And surviving
So that you may fall into love's warm embrace
Yet again
Only this time
You will be stronger
And wiser
And able
To see true love
As she wishes to be seen…

*Entangled Hearts*
# Beautiful I Am

My skin soft as satin,
Creamy like butter
And the color of toasted almonds.
I smile, staring at my reflection in the mirror
Wondering what beauty, true beauty is.
Gazing into my own eyes,
Trying to peek into my spirit,
I see a sleek brown face staring back at me
With a hazel speck in her right pupil.
An attention seeker, that spot is.
A birthmark, if you're wondering also.
More than just a color, my eyes sing.
They sing of understanding, they sing of compassion
But mostly, my eyes sing of love.
See, my eyes have glimpsed love once
But only briefly.
We got along real good too.
My eyes stared love in her cocoa brown face
And studied her.
Wanted to know why she came my way,
What did I do to deserve her gracious presence?
Calmly she said to me in the quietest tones,

*"Your heart called out to me*
*With the most beautiful song*
*Yet underneath*
*I heard soft, subtle whimpers of pain.*
*A pain you tried hard to bury*
*So that love could find you,*
*And it has.*
*You need not hold on to the pain anymore.*
*Your spirit wishes to only sing the songs of love.*
*Sensuous notes that softens men's ears*
*Like the smoothest silks and satin*
*And I am here to help you."*

## *Entangled Hearts*

With that the vision in the mirror faded
And I stood there,
Staring at myself,
Wondering at how beautiful I am…

*Entangled Hearts*
# Farewell

My chocolate knight
Dressed seductively sweet
In the creamiest of vanilla white tuxedos.
Always enhancing the beat of my heart
With just a glance.
I see you standing amid a beautiful garden
Full of fragrant flowers and singing birds
And I smile
Knowing this time is different somehow.
Things between us
Will never again be the same
Yet a part of me is content that you found happiness
Even though it's not with me.
Seeing that twinkle in your eyes
One last time
I stare, burning that vision of you
In my memory
For the rest of my days.
Blowing the softest kiss your way
I whisper,
*"Farewell my love…"*

*Entangled Hearts*
# I Loved Him

Not trusting myself,
In the beginning,
I held back.
When I opened completely
Our time was drastically short.
Hurt,
I rushed on
Determined to find that loving feeling again.
Finding an echo of that love
I held fast to it
Because I loved **him**.
Fighting my hurt,
Trudging on,
Determined to make **this** love work
I began to feel my spirit die
Because I loved **him**.
With a new awakening
And an open admittance
That I still loved **him**
My spirit felt renewed
Until I realized
Far too late
That I was far too late
Because I loved **him**.
Blessed through my hurt
I see daily
That had I not loved **him**
These words,
My spirit's words
Would not exist.

## About the Author

*Born and raised in North Philadelphia,*
*Why Yet found comfort in the*
*words of Maya Angelou's Gather Together In My Name.*
*From that book*
*sprang an interest in everything Maya Angelou,*
*including her poem*
*Phenomenal Woman.*
*Inspired at the age of thirteen,*
*Why Yet began*
*writing her own poems.*

*It wasn't until thirteen years later that she*
*found the courage to publish her collection of poetry,*
*Entangled Hearts where she discovered how*
*much of her words touched people's lives.*

*After a nine year hiatus, The Author Yani*
*(A Thug's Redemption Series)*
*convinced Why Yet to come out of*
*retirement and re-release*
*Entangled Hearts.*
*Her journey continues... Why Yet? Why not?*

*Entangled Hearts*

www.ingramcontent.com/pod-product-compliance
Lightning Source LLC
Chambersburg PA
CBHW031415040426
42444CB00005B/570